ALL I NEED IS YOU

PENNY HEFLEBOWER, PH. D

A BOOK OF HOPE AND

ENCOURAGEMENT

ISBN# 978-1-952963-03-2

Scripture quotes from the Thompson Chain-Reference Bible

New International Version

Copyright @ 1990 by

The B. B. Kirkbride Bible Company, Inc.

DEDICATION

I dedicate this book to three men who have had a huge influence in my life.

The first, was my father Warren Leonard Rebstad. Because of him I grew up learning about God and now have a personal relationship with him.

The second most important man in my life was my husband, David Ernest Heflebower. We were married for forty-eight years. In that time his love and affection for me was endless. And he showed me how to love others unconditionally.

The third person that has influenced my life is Sir Clyde Rivers. He has been my pastor since 2011. It was Dr. Rivers who taught me about the Kingdom of God, and what my purpose was here on earth. Dr. Rivers is always uplifting and encouraging everyone around him. He told me, "Make sure people leave you feeling better about themselves than when they came." I will never forget that.

Thank you to my three heroes.

FOREWORD

Foreword: Sir Clyde Rivers

World Civility Leader

This book is truly a practical masterpiece on how to have a relationship with God. Dr. Penny, has created the ability to show the simplicity of communicating with God on a day-to-day relationship basis. I recommend this book for anyone just starting their walk with God or someone who is seasoned and forgotten the simplicity of God.

Dr. Penny is truly a genius and as you read this book you will see the genius of simplicity that has been created. Penny has walked with God for 63 years and you will see the practicality and the experience of knowing God for all those years and this will make your experience easier as you read this masterpiece.

Table of Contents

I FOUND A FRIEND

———◆———

Whaat is the definition of friend?

"A person whom one knows and with whom one has a bond of mutual affection, with whom they spend a lot of time with."

I would like to introduce you to someone I met when I was seven-years-old. He's my closest friend and his name is Jesus. I invited him to come into my heart and be my forever friend. I believed then, and still do today, that because he died on the cross for my sins, and rose again that I will be with him in heaven someday. That gives me great hope.

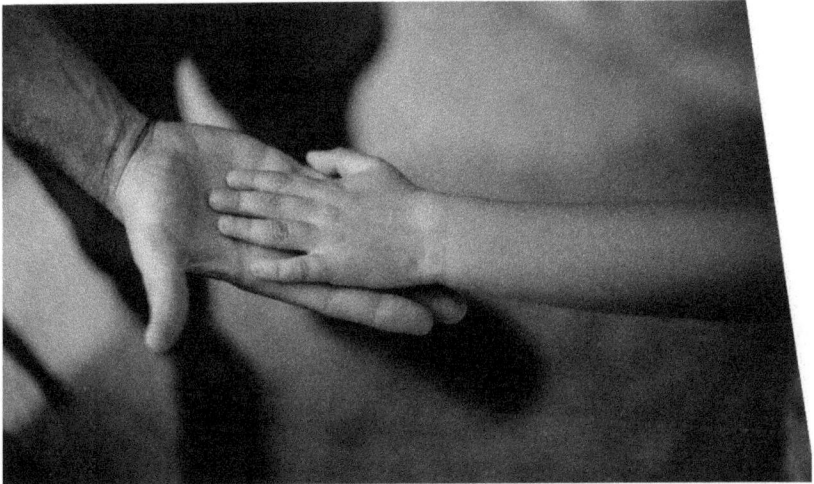

He is always there when I need him and I know he hears my prayers. Like all friendships it took time to get to really know him.

I realized that I needed him in my life, and that's when I began to fully trust him. His words are encouraging, uplifting, and always true.

"GODS STRENGTH IS LIMITLESS"

1. Do you have a friend that is always there for you and ready to help?

   _____

   _____

2. When was the last time you spent quality time with your friend?

   _____

   _____

3. When was the last time you spent quality time with God?

   _____

   _____

As the years went by our friendship grew. The more I got to know him the more I loved him, but I wasn't sure if he really loved me. Because you see, there were many times in my life when I said or did things that I know hurt and disappointed him. But it doesn't matter what we do or say he still loves us unconditionally and wants to be our friend.

This journey through life is tough, but we don't have to go through it alone. God promised he would never leave us or forsake us. That means that he is always around, we just need to call out to him. He is our shepherd.

Psalms 23

23:1 *The Lord is my shepherd; I shall not be in want.*

23:2 *He makes me lie down in green pastures; he leads me beside quiet waters.*

23:3 *He restores my soul. He guide's me in paths of righteousness for his name's sake.*

23:4 *Even though I walk through the valley of the shadow of death, I will fear no evil, for you are with me; your rod and your staff, they comfort me.*

23:5 *You prepare a table before me in the presence of my enemies. You anoint my head with oil; my cup overflows.*

23:6 *Surely goodness and love will follow me all the days of my life, and I will dwell in the house of the Lord forever. Amen*

He was always there for me

You've heard the saying "A dog is

man's best friend". Well, I say

God is man's best friend.

I NEEDED GOD WHEN I WAS GROWING UP

There are three girls in my family. My youngest sister had an infection on her face when she was just weeks old. To stop the infection the doctors used radiation treatments. The treatments did stop the infection but it also damaged my sister's brain, which meant she would never be normal again.

I didn't know it at the time but growing up in a family with a disabled sibling was God's way of preparing me for what he wanted me to become.

He was teaching me *patience*.

My older sister (Gloria) and I saw how much time and energy my mother spent taking care of our baby sister. So we had to have patience to get help with things that we needed and wanted. We also didn't get to spend a lot of time with our mom.

Gloria and I have always been close as sisters, and she is also my best friend. We not only looked out for each other, but we were taught to trust and rely on God to help us.

But most of all I learned what true love was.

Despite all that my parents went through in caring for my sister Alice, they took the time to teach us about God and his love. We didn't have much according to the world's standards, but we definitely knew we were loved.

The bible tells us that God is Love. If we follow his example and do what his Word says, we will be sharing love to the world.

1 Corinthians 13:13

"And now these three remain: faith, hope and love. But the greatest of these is Love."

I NEEDED GOD

WHEN I GOT MARRIED.

Church was a big part of my life growing up, and that's why it's no surprise that that's where I met my husband to be. He was in the United States Air Force when we got married and was stationed at a base in Puerto Rico. After our honeymoon here in California, we set up housekeeping in this faraway country.

Being only 19-years-old living in a place where most everyone spoke Spanish, in a house off base, alone all day while my husband was at work. The word that comes to mind is HOMESICK.

Although I was working and had my own car before I got married, I was still living at home with my folks. So, moving thousands of miles away from friends and family was hard.

Here I was in this foreign country all alone during the day, with nothing to do except clean the house and listen to Bobby Vinton singing "Mr. Lonely". I needed someone to talk to and something to occupy my time.

TRUST GOD AND DON'T BE AFRAID

1. Can you remember the last time you felt all alone?

_____

_____

2. What did it take to make you feel better?

_____

_____

I realized that I needed a closer relationship with God. He was there all the time. The problem was I didn't always include him in my day. You see, God won't force Himself on you. He is patiently waiting for you to come to him.

God created the whole earth so we don't have to worry about the future. We just need to have faith and trust in God. He will supply all your needs at just the right time.

WHY WORRY WHEN YOU CAN PRAY

Example - I didn't know that after my husband retired from the military, that I would have to go to work to help support the family. I hadn't work away from the home for many years, and frankly I didn't even know where to start looking.

A friend suggested looking into being an instructional aide for Special Education. So, I did. I was on a sub list for several months then God helped me get a part-time job closer to home. Through this whole job experience God was teaching me how to have patience and to have more confidence in myself. He was also helping me to learn to trust in him.

Six months later I applied for a full-time position with benefits, and got it. I ended up working with Special Need students for almost 19 years before I retired. This all happened because God provided.

I Needed God When My Husband Had A Stroke

He was only forty-seven years old when he retired from the military. Not knowing what kind of job to apply for, he decided to go to seminary to become a Pastoral Counselor. It was in his last year of seminary that he had a massive brain-stem stroke.

We were at a restaurant about to eat dinner when I noticed my husband trying to talk. I went over to him and he whispers to me that he couldn't swallow. I immediately rushed him to the emergency room. They admitted him and ran many tests trying to find the problem. After a week of no answers the Dr. sent him to a specialist at Cedar Sini Hospital in Beverly Hills, California. That day they found the blockage in his brain and could proceed with treatment.

I took the next two weeks off work to be with my husband. This was so frightening for all of us, not knowing if your loved one would ever walk, talk, or even eat again. It was because of friends & family praying for our situation that we made it through. I could feel the presence of God there in the hospital room. Sweet peace.

HAVE FAITH NOT FEAR

1. When was the last time you were in a situation where you didn't think you could keep going?

_____

_____

2. How did you solve the problem? Did you get help?

_____

_____

The journey of recovery was long. We had many home visits, rehab, and lots of Doctor's appointments. It was especially hard for me because I needed to go back to work, but my heart's desire was to be home and take care of my husband. This went on for fourteen years. Then I retired.

I had to rely on God and his strength to get me through each day.

Most people put on clothes soon after arising from bed. Similarly, the sooner you "put on God" by communicating with him, the better prepared you are for whatever comes your way. For me, getting up an hour earlier to spend time with God was well worth it.

I felt like I could handle anything that came my way that day. And I did, because I knew the Holy Spirit was always with me, guiding me.

JOURNEY TOGETHER TOWARD HEAVEN

I NEEDED GOD WHEN MY HUSBAND PASSED AWAY.

How do you say goodbye to someone you've been married to for forty-eight years?

A person who helped you raise two children and spent over 21 years in the United States Air Force together.

The first ten years after my husband retired from the USAF was rough, trying to adjust to a new lifestyle. Dave worked hard to make a living for his family, but God had other plans for him/us. God wanted us to start a Rescue Mission in southern California's High Desert, just northeast of Los Angeles.

Through much prayer and searching for God's wisdom and knowledge on how to accomplish this, we became the founders of the Victor Valley Rescue Mission.

Helping those who are hurting, hopeless and lost has always been my husband's passion. Taking this step of faith was the hardest thing we ever did, but it has also been the most rewarding.

It took a lot of prayer, volunteers, and just putting one foot in front of the other. But we were obedient to God. And now, over twenty years later the Mission is still open and helping thousands of people every month.

FIGHT YOUR BATTLES BY

PRAISING GOD

Because of exposure to Agent Orange, a toxic defoliant sprayed in Vietnam when Dave was there during the war. Dave's health slowly started to decline. He had many years of increasing medical problems, but it was in July of 2017 that he fell and fractured his back.

By this time his mind was slowly slipping away. He spent a week in the hospital for his back, then the next six months in a rehab hospital mainly because of his mental state. I went to visit him three times a week while he was there.

Sometimes he remembered me, and sometimes not. I can remember coming home to an empty house after those visits and just crying. Crying because I was physically and emotionally tired. Crying because I was losing my best friend and lover. And crying because I knew he was dying.

It was during those six months that God was preparing me to live alone. In Dec. of 2017 I was able to bring my husband home. With the help of the hospice team, I had two more months with my beloved. He passed away in his sleep in Feb. 2018.

1. *Have you ever lost a loved one? How did you cope?*

_____

_____

2. *Who did you go to for help and encouragement?*

_____

_____

The moment that he passed I cried because he went peacefully, and because his battle was over. He was now in the arms of Jesus and once again whole. I wouldn't have made it through that time without the presence of God in my life, and the help of my sister Gloria and friends.

When you are sitting all alone in an empty house wondering what to do next, that's when you cry out to God. It's as simple as saying, "Jesus Help Me". He hears you and will be there for you every time. He is just waiting for you to talk to him. We are his children; his creation and he is our heavenly father. All we need is God.

I Needed God When My Father Passed Away.

I grew up being a daddy's girl. He would often ask me to help with different projects that he was working on, even though he didn't really need my help. It made me feel important and needed.

One of the fondest memories that I have of my dad was going camping at San Clementi State Beach in southern California. Back in the day you were on a first-come, first-serve list to get a campsite.

You had to be present for roll call each day. So, Dad and I would go down before the rest of the family to reserve a spot. We packed up our 1958 Plymouth station wagon and slept in the car at night because we couldn't afford to stay in a motel. I remember going to the coffee shop and getting hot coco and a donut for breakfast. Wow, what a treat. Those were special bonding times for dad and I.

My dad taught us by example and not just words. He was faithful in having his time alone with God every day. And the most important thing I remember about my dad is that he was always there for me when I needed to talk. That's just like God!

LIVE LIKE YOU'RE LOVED

BECAUSE YOU ARE.

I feel so fortunate to have had my parents in my life until I was in my early 60's. Dad had Parkinson's Disease and passed away a year after mom. Because I was so close to my dad, I didn't know how I could ever live without him in my life.

1. Have you ever lost a loved one?

_____

_____

2. How did you handle the grief?

_____

_____

I was with dad the morning he passed. It was about six a.m. when I read to him from a devotional book, "Jesus Calling" which said:

"You are safe and secure in my presence. You are on your way to heaven; nothing can prevent you from reaching that destination."

Two hours later he was gone.

God gave me such a peace in my heart because of what I read to dad that day. And I know I will see my pop in heaven someday! With God, all things are possible. He makes a way where there is no way. We just need to trust him and obey.

WHO IS THE GOD OF HEAVEN?

———⊱✦⊰———

H e is a Spirit being who loves and cares about everyone and everything. He is Almighty God who created the heavens, the earth, and everything on the earth including man. This world is not our forever home, we are just passing through.

7.8 billion people are here on earth for a reason. God created each one of us with special gifts to be used for His purpose. It is important for us to stay connected to God so that he can lead and guide us through each day. How do we do that? We focus on what God's word (the bible) says, and then obey it.

How to talk to the King

Most of us have never had an opportunity to speak to a real king before. But if you did, what would you say? How would you act? Would you be scared or afraid that you might say the wrong thing?

When I was a little girl, I was taught to pray to God with my hands folded and my eyes closed. Because it showed reverence for God.

Through the years I have realized that God hears my prayers whether I think them, sing them, or pray them. He just wants his children to talk to him.

God is a spirit. And he knows your heart. He knows you because he created you. And he desires to have a personal relationship with you. That can only happen if you talk to him.

Out of religion into the

kingdom

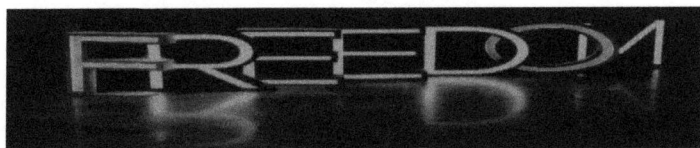

There are so many religions out there today. In the United States alone there are more than 26,000 different religions. Each one has its own set of rules and standards to go by. Let me ask you one question.

Where in the bible does it say that Jesus started a religion? For the answer to that question lets go to God's word.

*Isaiah 9:6-7 "For to us a child is born, to us a son is given, and the government will be on his shoulders. And he will be called Wonderful Counselor, Mighty God, Everlasting Father, Prince of Peace. (7) Of the increase of his government and peace there will be no end. He will reign on David's throne and over his kingdom, establishing and upholding it with justice and righteousness from that time on and forever. The zeal of the Lord almighty will accomplish this."

Here we see that the government, the kingdom, will be on God's shoulders and that there will be no end to his reign. This is security and hope for the future.

*Matthew. 6:33 "But seek first his kingdom and his righteousness and all these things will be given to you."

- A Kingdom concept is something that God invented. God was the first king. And he produced the idea when he created the heavens and the earth. Heaven is an invisible country where God lives and is King.

- He wanted to extend his kingdom, so he created another universe. He also created his children to be kings here on the earth, which makes him the King of Kings.

- Kingdoms have citizens, Religion has members.

- God created a government for his citizens to live in, not a religion. In the kingdom of God, we have dominion and the Holy Spirit works with us. In religion you have to do all the work.

- When Citizens of God's Kingdom speak the angels move.

"WE ARE MADE IN GOD'S IMAGE"

GENISUS 1:26

IT'S NEVER TOO LATE TO CHANGE

All my life I have been trying to figure out what my purpose is here on earth. "Why was I born"? You know, that thing that fulfills you. Makes you feel complete.

I finally realized what God wanted me to do for him at the age of sixty-three. You're never too old to serve God. "When the world thought I was on my way out, I was just getting started."

GOD GAVE ME WHAT I NEEDED WHEN I NEEDED IT

My life was renewed after my husband passed away. I know that sounds strange, but it's true. My husband and I spent over 21 years in the military. After he retired, I needed to go to work to help make ends meet.

From the time I was married at nineteen, until the age of sixty-three I was a mother, wife, sister, daughter, and good friend, However, I didn't know who I was as a person or what I was supposed to become. Does this sound weird?

1. What are your dreams and desires?

_____

_____

2. If you could do or be anything you wanted to be, what would it be?

_____

_____

3. How can you achieve those dreams?

_____

_____

WHAT RESOURCES HAS GOD GIVEN YOU?

I never had or took the time to find out who I was, what I liked, or what I wanted to be when I grew up. My kids are all grown now and involved with their own lives. After my husband passed away, I asked myself, "Now what"?

Now I was free to be me. After grieving the loss of my husband, and much prayer, God revealed to me what my purpose for living was. Actually, there are several.

I FINALLY FOUND WHERE I BELONGED

One of my purposes in life is to bring Honor, Love and

Encouragement to the Differently Abled people of the world.
This will happen through an organization called

<u>"Challenged Champions and Heroes."</u>

In 2015 I was asked to join the organization as Vice President of Communications. Nothing gives me more joy and happiness than to see a smile on the faces of God's created ones.

As I mentioned earlier, I grew up with a sister whose brain was damaged from radiation. Growing up with Alice has given me a heart to want to help and love those people who don't fit into the world's systems. I believe that every life is valuable. We all need each other in some way or another.

My sister Alice

Another passion of mine is sharing the Kingdom of God with the world.

I heard the Kingdom messages in 2013 and they changed my life forever. I understood why we were born and what our purpose is. It's to serve God and bring Him glory. I want people to know who the God of Heaven is and what he can and will do for them.

1. What resources or gifts has God given you?

_____

_____

2. How can you use those resources to help others
   and bring Glory to God?

_____

_____

One last thing that I have found very fulfilling, has been hosting foreign exchange students in my home.

I learned about several organizations after my husband passed away. It gives me so much pleasure to interact with these young people, and I look forward to them coming. So far, I have had students from China, Japan, Germany, France and Russia.

I love learning all about their different customs and lifestyles. Likewise, they have so many questions about our western culture. One thing that they all love is going to church with me and they especially love the music.

I hope that this book has brought some hope and encouragement into your life. I pray God's blessings on you.

GOD IS READY TO MEET YOUR NEEDS

———⬡———

ARE YOU READY TO MEET GOD?

www.ingramcontent.com/pod-product-compliance
Lightning Source LLC
LaVergne TN
LVHW011338080426
835513LV00006B/430